# LEGACIES OF INDUSTRIAL REVOLUTION

## STEAM ENGINE AND TRANSPORTATION

## HISTORY BOOK FOR KIDS

## CHILDREN'S HISTORY

BABY PROFESSOR

EDUCATION KIDS

Speedy Publishing LLC
40 E. Main St. #1156
Newark, DE 19711
www.speedypublishing.com
Copyright 2017

In this book, we're going to talk about steam engines and transportation. So, let's get right to it!

The steam engine was one of the most important new inventions that came out of the era of the Industrial Revolution. Although the Industrial Revolution had started before the perfection of the steam engine, without it, the technology and inventions of that era wouldn't have progressed as quickly as they did.

STEAM ENGINE

# HOW DOES A STEAM ENGINE OPERATE?

An engine that runs on steam operates using steam created from boiling water. To make the steam, coal was burned to heat the water to the boiling point.

The hot steam created from the boiling water would move pistons within cylinders. The movement of the pistons in the cylinders provides power to a machine or is used to rotate a wheel.

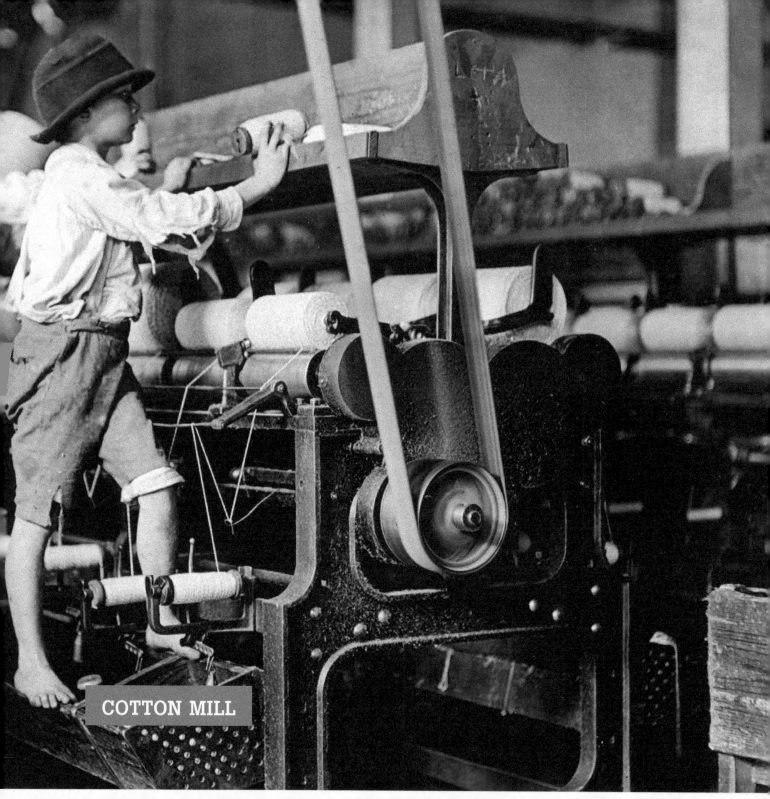

COTTON MILL

# WHY WAS THE STEAM ENGINE IMPORTANT?

Prior to the advent of steam power, manufacturing facilities and textile mills needed to be powered by wind or water. Supplies had to be brought to the locations by men or beasts of burden. Although water was a good use of power, the factories were limited in terms of the locations where they could be built since a fast-moving river had to be nearby.

Depending on the weather, wind and water weren't always reliable. During times of drought, water wasn't moving or unavailable and during the winter, the water would freeze. Wind power depended on the weather as well. Once practical steam power was available, factories could be located at any site.

STEAMBOAT

The steam engine was able to power huge machines. As it evolved, it was used in many different applications from running machines in factories and mines to powering transportation, such as trains and steamboats.

# THE HISTORY OF THE STEAM ENGINE

The ancient Greeks knew about the power of steam but it was sixteen hundred years after that discovery when steam was first used to power engines. Prior to that time, beasts of burden had to be used to transport supplies.

COAL MINE

In the 17th century, glassmakers in Britain needed vast amounts of fuel in the form of coal to keep their furnaces stoked to produce glass. The system that was being used was one that was dependent on slow-moving horses and pulleys to drain the water out of the coal mines so the coal could be extracted. They needed a better way to do this faster and they offered money to any scientist who could figure it out.

In the year 1698, Thomas Savery, an inventor from Britain, invented a pump that was powered by steam. The steam in the pump created a vacuum and was able to pull the water up vertically through a pipe. The theory behind this invention had been around for many centuries, but had never been made practical.

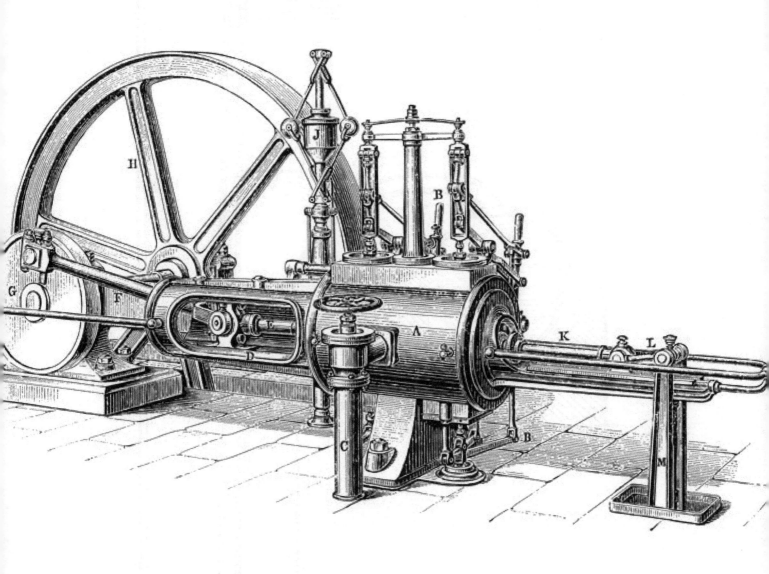

OLD STEAM MACHINE

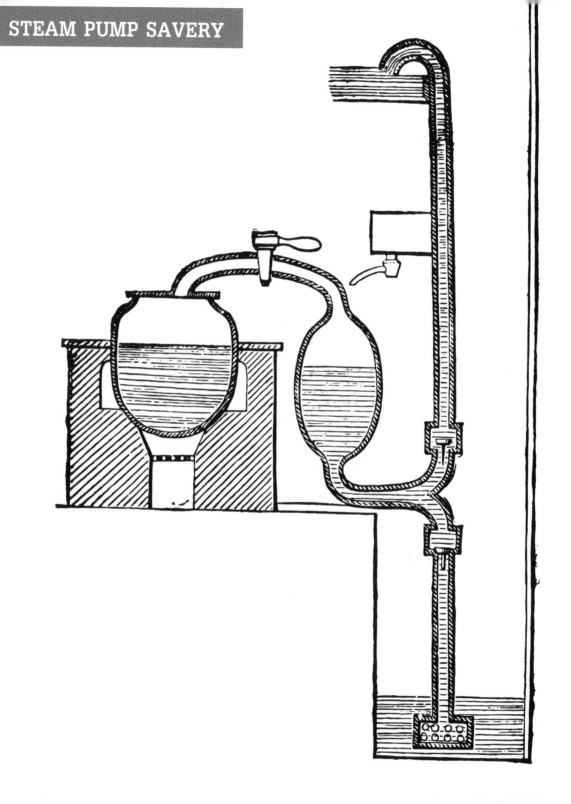

A blacksmith by trade, Thomas Newcomen, improved on Savery's pump in 1712 through the use of pistons as well as cylinders. Newcomen's engine was quickly used to pump water out of mines.

Then, in 1778, James Watt improved the design of the steam engine dramatically with the help of his business partner Matthew Boulton. The men installed hundreds of new steam engines in factories. The Boulton and Watt steam engine was more compact and didn't need as much coal to power it. Soon, everyone knew about this speedy engine and by the early part of the 1800s, it was operating in factories in Great Britain. Watt coined the term "horsepower" so he could explain to potential customers how much power his engine could produce compared to the power of horses. It was a brilliant marketing decision because it helped people to understand the power of his engines very quickly.

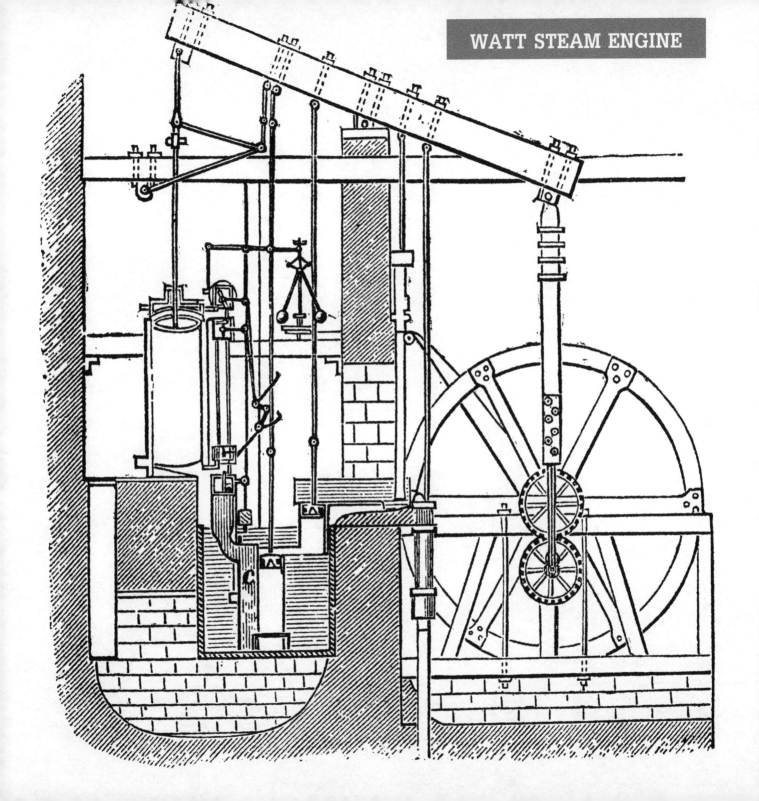

WATT STEAM ENGINE

Throughout the next hundred years, different inventors worked to improve steam engines.

Their designs were adapted for many different types of applications from running large machines in mills to transportation uses such as powering locomotives and steamboats.

# CHANGES IN TRANSPORTATION

The Industrial Revolution completely transformed how people and goods were moved from one place to another. Before the steam engine, men had to rely on beasts of burden to pull carts or wagons. Boats were used on waterways but they weren't very fast. Travel of all types was very slow and arduous. To travel from the east coast to the west coast of the United States took months. Once the steam engine was adapted for powering transportation this all changed. The first of these changes was the way boats were powered.

STEAM RIVERBOAT

# STEAMBOATS ON THE RIVER

Boats to transport goods by waterways had been used since ancient times. They were great for traveling downstream with the current, but when they had to go upstream it was a challenge. Men could use oars to travel against the current and wind power could sometimes be harnessed to speed up boats on their travels.

However, once the steam engine was invented, the problem of moving quickly against the current was solved.

Robert Fulton, an American inventor, who had built submarines before, created the first practical steamboat that could be used for commercial purposes in 1807. This boat could travel against the current upstream through the power of its steam engine.

It didn't take long for steamboats to be carrying people and supplies along the waterways of the United States. At the beginning, the boilers on steamboats were dangerous and sometimes exploded. In fact, the brother of famous author Mark Twain, Henry Clemens, was killed by a steamboat boiler explosion.

STEAM BOILER

ERIE CANAL

# THE BIRTH OF CANALS

Depending on where natural waterways existed, they didn't always easily connect to each other. In order to make the connections easier, manmade canals were built. The Erie Canal was designed to create a route via water from the New York City coastline and the Atlantic Ocean to the Mideast's Great Lakes. When construction was completed in the year 1825, at 363 miles in length it was second only to China's Grand Canal.

It was important both for commerce and travel and increased New York's prosperity. It gave the port of New York a huge advantage over other ports in the United States. There was also a surge of canal building in Britain as well. By the year 1850, more than 4,000 miles of waterway – connecting canals had been constructed there.

ERIE CANAL

# THE RAILROADS ARE BUILT

Even better for transportation than steamboats and the building of canals, was the advent of the steam locomotive. Trains weren't limited by natural or artificial waterways. Of course, tracks had to be built to get trains from one place to another and there were sometimes waterways or mountains to cross.

The first practical steam locomotive was built by Richard Trevithick in 1804. Unfortunately, it was so massive and heavy that it broke its rails after three trips. However, by 1808, Trevithick had built a locomotive that carried passengers on a circular track in London.

STEPHENSON'S ROCKET

In 1829, Robert Stephenson's steam locomotive called the Rocket was used to pull railway cars from Liverpool to Manchester in the United Kingdom. The railway was a success and soon train tracks were being built all over Europe.

Around 1830, railways were being designed and built in the eastern region of the United States. One of the first was the Baltimore and Ohio railway. Its first section was launched in 1830. In less than 40 years, the first railway that connected the east coast to the west coast was completed.

# TRANSCONTINENTAL RAILROAD

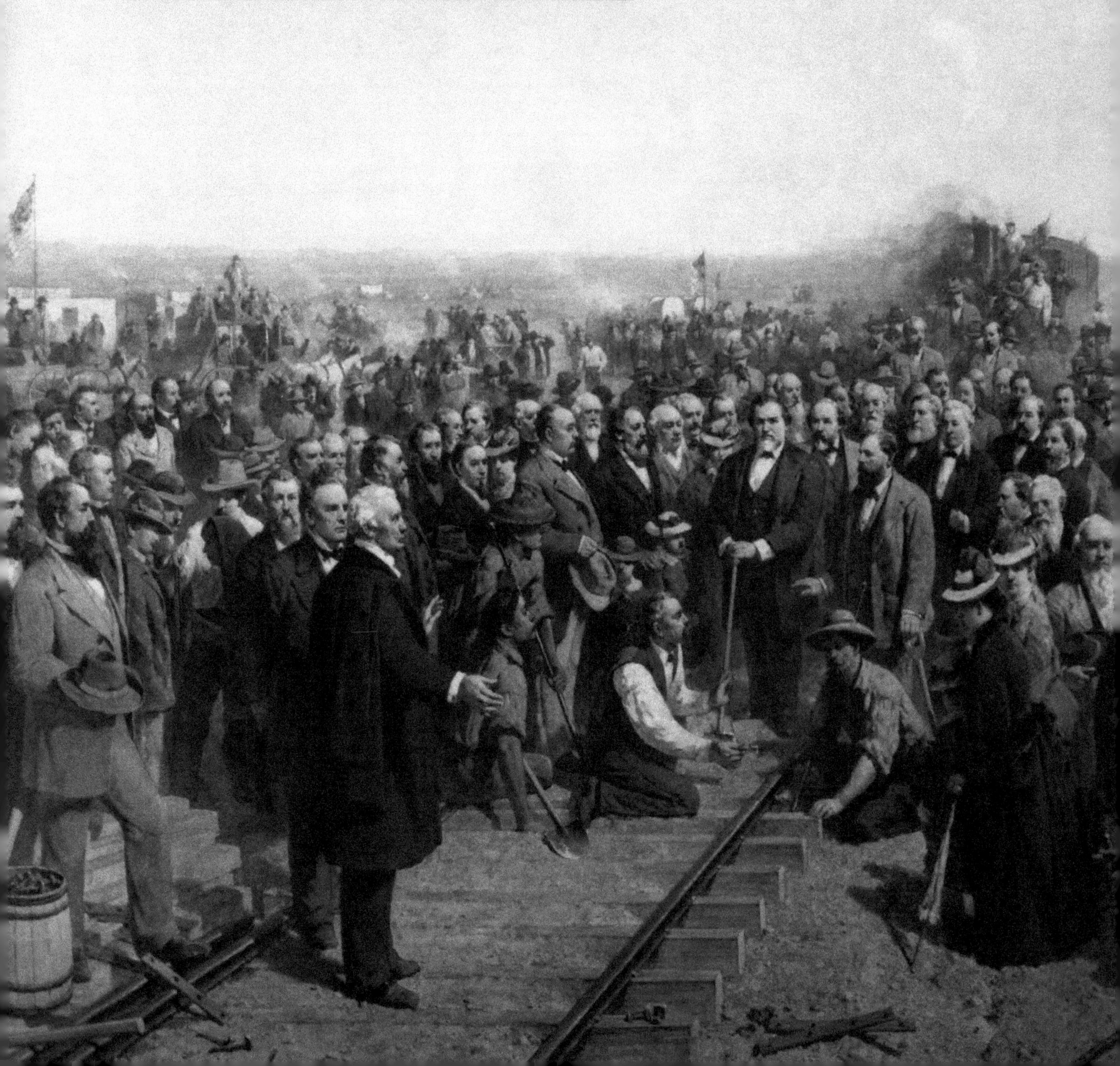

This First Transcontinental Railroad completely changed the vast expanse of the United States and made it "smaller" in a sense. Before the railways were in place, it would take months to travel from one coast to the other. The west coast seemed like a world apart from the east. The railway changed all that. In the 1870s, people and supplies could be transported coast to coast in a few days.

# IMPROVED ROAD CONSTRUCTION

Even with these new forms of transportation there were still gaps and people still needed to use roads to get from place to place in horse-drawn carriages. Prior to the Industrial Revolution, roads were sometimes just made of dirt and they weren't maintained well at all. However, getting from place to place at a speedier pace than before became more important. A new process called "macadam," which allowed workers to create smooth roads made from gravel was introduced.

MACADAM

MODERN TRAIN

# ARE STEAM ENGINES STILL IN USE TODAY?

Most train engines today are powered by electricity or internal combustion engines that use either gas or diesel. There are a few places in the world that still use steam engines to power their trains and there are also antique locomotives for entertainment.

Steamboats are generally used for entertainment. Factories around the world still use steam power. Power plants that generate nuclear power use fusion to create steam to produce electrical current.

# INDUSTRIAL REVOLUTION AND ITS LEGACIES

During the Industrial Revolution there were many different inventions that had a huge impact. The invention of the steam engine made it possible to power machines in factories and completely changed transportation worldwide, both by steamboat and by trains run by steam locomotives.

Awesome! Now that you've read about steam engines and transportation, you may want to read more about trains in the Baby Professor book Why Do Trains Stay on Track? Train Books for Kids.

Visit

**BABY PROFESSOR**
EDUCATION KIDS

# www.BabyProfessorBooks.com

to download Free Baby Professor eBooks
and view our catalog of new and exciting
Children's Books

Lightning Source UK Ltd.
Milton Keynes UK
UKHW051505300819
348842UK00006B/189/P